CHICAGO PUBLIC LIBRARY . Humboldt Park Branch
1605 N. Troy Street . Chicago . Illinois . 60647
Telephone . 312-744-2244
Library Hours
Monday-Thursday, 9 am- 8 pm
Friday & Saturday, 9 am-5 pm
Sunday, closed

BIG

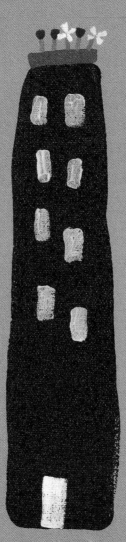
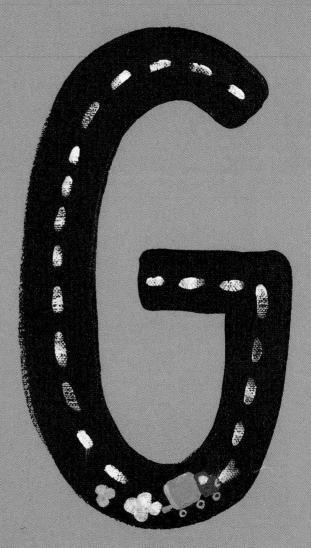

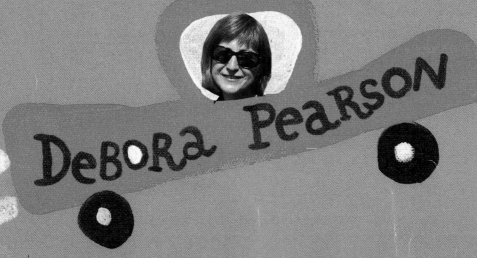

DeBoRa PeaRSON

CITY SONG

LYNN ROWE REED

TAXI

GO

Holiday House / New York

For David and Lynn Bennett, my agents.
Thank you for all you do.
D. P.

To Micayla, Carter and Collin
L. R. R.

Printed in the United States of America
The text typeface is Catseye Medium.
The art for this book was created with acrylic paint on canvas.
www.holidayhouse.com
First Edition
1 3 5 7 9 10 8 6 4 2

Library of Congress Cataloging-in-Publication Data
Pearson, Debora.
Big city song / by Debora Pearson ; illustrated by Lynn Rowe Reed.— 1st ed.
p. cm.
Summary: Rhyming text describes the many sounds of the city.
ISBN-13: 978-0-8234-1988-3 (hardcover)
ISBN-10: 0-8234-1988-6 (hardcover)
[1. City and town life—Fiction. 2. Sound—Fiction. 3. Noise—Fiction.
4. Stories in rhyme.] I. Reed, Lynn Rowe, ill. II. Title.
PZ8.3.P274714Big 2006
[E]—dc22
2005021786

Photograph of
Debora Pearson
on the left side of
the title page spread
by Michael Fattori.

Photograph of
Lynn Rowe Reed on
the right side of the title
page spread by Brian Art.

Sun comes up. . . .

Sweep! Sweep! Sweep!

Dusty little street cleaner swishes down the street.

Bundles of newspapers thump off a truck.

Fountain s-s-s-s-s-s-spurts on.

Pigeons flap up.

Man walks his dog–dog walks his man.

Cars in a conga line lurch, chuff—**STOP**.

Trucks start to bellow. Drivers start to yell.

Ooh—yuck!

Trash truck starts to smell!

Police car whoop-whoops over.
Attention—do-si-do!
Around this way, swing left, veer right.

Now, all together . . .

Over at the work site, it's

Clonk!
Bonk!
Bash!

Demolition's
starting,
and it's going
to be a smash.

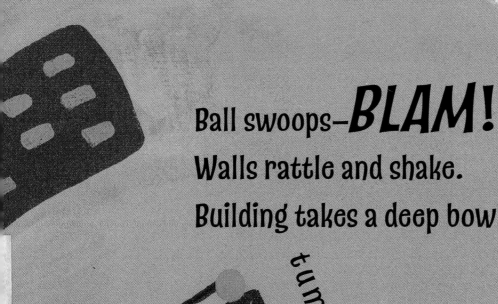

Ball swoops—*BLAM!*
Walls rattle and shake.
Building takes a deep bow . . .

tumbles and breaks.

BASH 'N' SMASH
COMPANY

Snack truck honks—now workers start to run.

Grab lunch, sit down, read a little news.
Listen to the radio—Chew! Chew! Chew!

Down at the park trees shimmy and sway.
They do a leafy hula dance—
shake! shake! shake!

Church bells *bing-bong* slow, sad songs.

Rhumba-ba-ba-BOOM!
Thunder sounds
like a drum.

Then raindrops tap-dance—
*tippa-tappa, tippa-tappa,
thrum, thrum,* THRUMMMM.

Faces in a bus
watch umbrellas bop and bob
as people leap and jump
over puddles—
Oops! *Ker-plop!*

Fog floats in.
Wipers *swish-clunk*.
Soggy man, soggy dog
slip, slide, rush.

Dash home, dry off, everyone needs food.

Dinner's ready, time to eat—Mmm, tastes good!

Full moon
glows like a
spotlight
way up high.

It shines on people

dancing . . .

reading . . .

singing lullabies.

Tiptoe off to bed.
Click out the lights.

Big city's calm..... Big city's quiet.....

EEEEE-O, eeeee-o, eeeee-o . . .
Clang-ang-ang-ang!
CRASH!

CALL 911

Someone's banging rhythms
with their lively little hands.

Can't you feel the midnight beat?
Just listen to the symphony of sounds on the street!